18

D0481452

EAT
YOUR
WORDS

Books by Charlotte Foltz Jones

Mistakes That Worked

Accidents May Happen

Fingerprints and Talking Bones

Eat Your Words

EAT YOUR WORDS

A FASCINATING LOOK AT THE LANGUAGE OF FOOD

Charlotte Foltz Jones

Illustrated by John O'Brien

Delacorte Press

The author gratefully acknowledges Lauri Hornik,

who knows how the cookie crumbles

and what to do with the crumbs.

All rights reserved. Published in the United States by Delacorte Press,
an imprint of Random House Children's Books, a division
of Penguin Random House LLC, New York.

Originally published in hardcover and in slightly different form by
Delacorte Press, an imprint of Random House Children's Books,
a division of Penguin Random House LLC, New York, in 1999.

Delacorte Press is a registered trademark and the colophon
is a trademark of Penguin Random House LLC.

Visit us on the Web! rhcbooks.com

Educators and librarians, for a variety of teaching tools,
visit us at RHTeachersLibrarians.com

Library of Congress Cataloging-in-Publication Data is available upon request.
ISBN 978-1-5247-6681-8 (trade)—ISBN 978-1-5247-6686-3 (ebook)

The text of this book is set in 11-point Garth Graphic.
Interior design by Ken Crossland

Printed in the United States of America
10 9 8 7 6 5 4 3 2 1
Updated Edition

Dedicated to
JOHN PAUL JONES,
who brings laughter to the table,
but who never has second helpings

CONTENTS

CHAPTER 6: TALKING TURKEY

CHAPTER 7: BY WORD OF MOUTH

EAT
YOUR
WORDS

THE MEAL BEGINS

In sadness and in joy, people eat.

In victory and defeat, people eat.

Before thinking, while thinking, and after thinking, people eat.

While meeting, reading, writing, waiting, riding, resting, listening, spending, watching, and touring . . . people eat.

Because food is necessary to survival, our entire culture is based on it. It's in our laws, our money, our superstitions, our celebrations, and especially our language.

This book is about the history of food-related words and phrases. It's *not* about nutrition, cooking, recipes, or kitchen safety. It's a shopping list of curious food etymology, and a menu of the origins of funny-sounding food. And to add spice, there is "food for thought"—tasty tidbits of trivia for the mind to chew.

Bon appétit! ("Enjoy your meal!")

CHAPTER 1

FOOD FOLKS

Some people leave their fingerprints
in the cake frosting.
Other people's names are on the menu.

Beef Stroganoff

The Stroganoff family was well known in Russia for hundreds of years. With their great wealth, they helped develop the Russian mining, fur, and timber industries.

One of the last prominent members of the family was the popular Count Paul Stroganoff. In the early 1800s he was a diplomat, a member of the court of Tsar Alexander III, and a member of the Imperial Academy of Arts.

He was also a gourmet who loved to entertain guests by hosting dinner parties. One of the dishes he often served was made with sautéed beef, onions, mushrooms, sour cream, and other condiments. This dish became known as beef Stroganoff.

Doesn't it seem odd that a family who contributed so much to a great country's development is remembered today for a beef dish served over noodles?

Caesar Salad

Caesar salad has *nothing* to do with the emperor who ruled Rome two thousand years ago.

The Caesar salad at your local café was originally called aviator salad.

In 1924 an American named Alex Cardini worked at his brother's restaurant in Tijuana, Mexico. One night, more customers than normal came in to eat, and the restaurant kitchen ran out of the usual menu items. So Alex put together odds and ends—eggs, romaine lettuce, Parmesan cheese, garlic, olive oil, lemon juice, and pepper. He made croutons out of some dried bread and then mixed everything together.

The customers loved it!

He named it aviator salad since the restaurant was near an airfield. Later the name was changed to Caesar salad after Alex's brother, who owned the restaurant.

Eggs Benedict

You won't find eggs Benedict on a fast-food menu. It's a very rich breakfast item made of English muffins, poached eggs, Canadian bacon, and hollandaise sauce.

There are two stories about the origin of eggs Benedict. Either might be true.

The first story: A wealthy lady named Mrs. LeGrand Benedict was having lunch at Delmonico's, a restaurant in New York City, one Saturday in the 1920s. She complained that there was "nothing new" on the menu.

The chef put together "something new." Mrs. Benedict was pleased, so the chef named it eggs Benedict.

The second story: Samuel Benedict, a New York socialite, had had too much to drink one night in 1894. He went into the Waldorf-Astoria the next morning and ordered his "perfect remedy for a hangover." It was such a great combination that the hotel's restaurant added it to the menu and named it eggs Benedict.

Graham Crackers

Sylvester Graham was a Presbyterian minister in Connecticut in the early 1800s. He was convinced that people were suffering from many bad habits, including poor diets.

He preached against tight clothing, soft mattresses, and alcohol. He thought pepper, mustard, and catsup caused insanity. He preached in favor of exercise, open bedroom windows, cold showers, and a vegetarian diet. He also recommended "cheerfulness at meals."

Graham is probably most remembered for his belief that white bread was evil and people should eat "unbolted" wheat flour (wheat flour from which the bran has not been removed). He urged women to stop buying bread from bakeries and instead to make their own.

This suggestion so infuriated professional bakers that a street fight once broke out in Boston after one of Graham's sermons.

But Graham had many followers. Graham societies formed, and Graham boardinghouses and Graham food stores opened.

Today health experts know that Sylvester Graham wasn't all wrong. People are exercising more, eating more vegetables, and using whole-wheat flour.

The graham cracker is still popular, although most commercial graham crackers are made with bleached flour, sugar, and preservatives—not the healthy ingredients the Reverend Sylvester Graham preached about.

S'MORES

4 graham crackers
4 regular-sized marshmallows
1 1.55-ounce milk chocolate bar

Preheat your oven to 400°F. Break the graham crackers in half and place them on a baking sheet. Place the marshmallows on half of the graham cracker portions. Break the chocolate bar into equal pieces and distribute those among the other graham cracker halves. Bake for 3 to 5 minutes. Carefully remove the sheet from the oven with mitts. Place one graham cracker half with chocolate on top of a graham cracker half with marshmallow. Do the same for the rest, serve, and enjoy.

Makes 4 s'mores.

Lobster Newburg

Lobster Newburg is a very expensive dish with a very funny history.

Ben Wenberg was a sea captain who traveled all over the world. On a trip to New York City in 1876 he brought a recipe he'd picked up in South America. He was given permission to prepare the lobster-and-cream dish in the kitchen of Delmonico's restaurant.

It was an instant hit. The chef added it to the dining room's menu and named it after the captain—lobster à la Wenberg.

Soon afterward, Ben Wenberg was involved in a huge brawl at the restaurant. In anger, the chef changed the name of the famous dish. So lobster à la Wenberg became lobster Newburg.

More than a hundred years later restaurants all over America still serve lobster Newburg.

Macadamia Nuts

Macadamia nuts could have been called von Mueller or Hill nuts. In 1857 two botanists, Ferdinand von Mueller and Walter Hill, were in the Australian bush country when they discovered a tree that had never been described in scientific terms before.

Von Mueller decided to name the tree after John MacAdam. MacAdam was a physician from Scotland who had come to Australia in 1855 to lecture and work. Von Mueller and MacAdam had become good friends.

Dr. MacAdam never tasted the macadamia nut and never even saw the tree that was named after him. He died of pleurisy while on board a ship bound for New Zealand in 1865.

Melba Toast and Peach Melba

Dame Nellie Melba, an opera singer from Australia, toured the world from 1887 to 1926.

While she was performing in London, she stayed at the Savoy Hotel. Trying to stay slim, she ordered thinly sliced toast.

One day someone in the kitchen sent out bread that appeared to be too thin and overtoasted. The waiter apologized, but Nellie loved it. Thus it was named melba toast.

Another well-known dish was named for this great singer. In 1892 the chef Georges-Auguste Escoffier attended one of Dame Nellie Melba's performances. Afterward he created a beautiful dessert in the shape of a swan, using peaches, vanilla ice cream, and crushed raspberries. He named the dessert peach Melba in her honor.

Reuben

This unique sandwich is made with corned beef, sauerkraut, and Swiss cheese on rye bread. Two Reubens share the credit for its creation.

Arnold Reuben operated a restaurant in New York City. The story goes that in 1914 an actress who was starring in a Charlie Chaplin film came into Arnold Reuben's restaurant and announced that she was very hungry and wanted a large combination.

The sandwich Arnold Reuben fixed for her was such a success that he named it after himself! This version of the Reuben used ham instead of corned beef.

Another story says that in 1955, at a weekly poker game in Omaha, Nebraska, the participants fixed their own sandwiches. One player, Reuben Kay, devised the combination of ingredients.

And this, most people agree, was the birth of the Reuben sandwich.

Salisbury Steak

It seems as if experts today are constantly changing their minds about what's good for us. It was the same in 1888.

Dr. James Salisbury was a British doctor who became well known as a health expert. He preached that eating well-cooked ground beef three times a day would cure tuberculosis, hardening of the arteries, gout, colitis, asthma, bronchitis, rheumatism, mental derangement, and pernicious anemia. He also recommended drinking a glass of warm water before and after each meal.

Other doctors laughed at Salisbury, but many people believed in his methods and followed his diet. His specially prepared meat became known as Salisbury steak.

Sandwiches

People have probably been eating a piece of meat between two slices of bread ever since bread was invented five thousand years ago. But this menu item didn't receive its name until 1762.

John Montagu, the Fourth Earl of Sandwich, was a gambler. One night he didn't want to leave the gaming tables even to eat, so he ordered his servants to quickly bring him some meat between slices of bread. That way, he would still have one hand free to play while he filled his stomach.

Today we continue to call his "fast food" a sandwich.

FOOD FOR THOUGHT

LAWS OF THE FOOD POLICE

Laws are not permanent. What's legal one day can be illegal the next. All these silly food laws were passed at one time, but some may have been repealed by now.

- In Joliet, Illinois, it is against the law to put cake in a cookie jar.
- Banana peels can't be tossed on the streets in Waco, Texas.
- Memphis, Tennessee, law prohibits the sale of bologna on Sunday.
- In California, it is illegal to peel an orange in a hotel room.
- It's a crime in Idaho to give your sweetheart a box of candy weighing less than fifty pounds.
- In Massachusetts, it is illegal to put tomatoes in clam chowder.
- Pennsville, New Jersey, has a law prohibiting anyone from selling baskets of fresh cucumbers within the town limits.

- Iowa state law makes it illegal to have a rotten egg in your possession.
- In Gary, Indiana, it is against the law to ride a bus or attend a theater within four hours after eating garlic.
- It is illegal to take a bite out of someone else's hamburger in Oklahoma.
- In Lexington, Kentucky, it is against the law to carry an ice cream cone in your pocket.
- In Greene, New York, it is illegal to eat peanuts and walk backward on the sidewalk while a concert is going on.

CHAPTER 2

FOOD ON THE MAP

There's plenty of food on the map: Bacon, Georgia;
Cherry, Nebraska; Rice, Minnesota; Hominy,
Oklahoma; Pine Apple, Alabama; Orange, Florida;
Orange, Indiana; and Orange, Texas, for starters.
Here's the right turn down the road to locations that
sound good enough to eat. This chapter is all about
places named for foods, and foods named for places.

Baked Alaska

It's a little tricky to bake ice cream inside a sponge cake
and still have it come out frozen. The secret: Spread a
meringue made of egg whites and sugar over and around
the ice cream before baking the ice cream and cake batter in the oven. The meringue serves as insulation so
that the heat doesn't melt the ice cream.

The science behind this dessert magic was discovered not by a baker but by an American physicist named
Benjamin Thompson in the late 1700s. The dessert

became a specialty of French, Chinese, and American chefs.

In French this dessert is called *omelette norvégienne,* which means "Norwegian omelette." The egg whites are the "omelette." The frozen ice cream represents the ice that was transported from the cold regions of Norway to European countries before ice machines were invented.

In the United States the dessert was previously known as Alaska-Florida—"Alaska" for the cold ice cream and "Florida" for the hot sponge cake. When the United States bought Alaska from Russia in 1867, the food was renamed baked Alaska in honor of the new territory.

OTHER FOOD USING REAL PLACE NAMES

- Belgian waffle
- Boston cream pie
- California roll
- French fries
- German chocolate cake
- Hawaiian shaved ice
- London broil
- Swedish meatballs
- Texas toast
- Worcestershire sauce

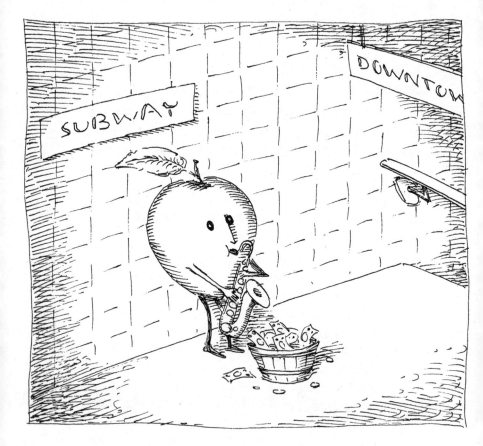

The Big Apple

The 8.5 million folks who live in New York City call their home the Big Apple. But how many of them know why?

There are at least six theories on how New York City became known as the Big Apple. The most accepted story says that jazz musicians created the term in the 1920s. The musicians wanted a nickname for the popular, booming place where they performed—the Big Town, the Big Time, the Main Stem, the Big Apple. New York City was the shiny apple at the top of the success tree.

The New York City Convention and Visitors Bureau began a promotional campaign in 1971 to attract tourists. They used the jazz musicians' nickname, and their campaign worked. Most people are now familiar with the Big Apple.

Bologna

Webster's New World Dictionary defines *bologna* as a large smoked sausage. Its American name comes from the city where it was first made: Bologna, Italy.

In Italy, the city is pronounced "bo-LO-nya" and the sausage is known as mortadella. But Americans call it baloney. Since this sausage was cheap, *baloney* became a term Americans used in the late 1800s to describe anything that had little value. By 1928 the term was so popular that presidential candidate Al Smith said during a 1936 speech, "No matter how thin you slice it, it's still baloney."

Buffalo Wings

They sound like part of some kind of mutant bird. But actually, this is a dish of chicken wings that was originally made in Buffalo, New York—Buffalo chicken wings, more commonly known as Buffalo wings.

Teressa Bellissimo and her husband ran the Anchor Bar in Buffalo, New York, in 1964. One night her son and his friends came in and wanted a snack. So Teressa mixed a new sauce for the chicken wings she had on hand. She added some celery and dipping sauce and served the snack.

Everyone loved the wings. Their popularity spread first across town and then across the nation. They became known as Buffalo wings, and today people everywhere ask for them.

FUN FACTS ABOUT BUFFALO WINGS

There is an annual Wing Bowl in Philadelphia, at which competitors try to eat the most wings. The record for most wings eaten is 444 wings in 26 minutes, set by Patrick Bertoletti.

The average American eats 90 chicken wings per year and roughly 12 at one sitting.

FUN FACTS ABOUT FIGS

There are no blossoms on fig tree branches. Instead, the blossom is inside the fruit.

The many little flowers produce the crunchy seeds, which give figs their unique texture.

Figs can help retain moisture in baked goods, keeping them fresher longer.

The most popular dipping sauce for chicken wings is ranch, with bleu cheese coming in second.

Each year on Super Bowl Sunday, Americans eat an average of 1.25 billion chicken wings. That many wings laid end to end would circle the Grand Canyon 120 time

The National Buffalo Wing Festival is an annual event held in Buffalo, New York, that attracts an average of 80,000 people.

Fig Newtons

In 1892 James Mitchell developed a machine that wrap cookie dough around a thick fig filling. Th nedy Biscuit Works in Cambridgeport, Massach purchased the machine and added the new trea line of crackers and cookies.

At the time, all the company's products were for nearby towns—Cambridge Salts, Shrewsbur con Hills, Melroses, and Harvards. When the fi first came onto the market, it was Newton's tur

Would a Fig Worcester or a Fig Lexington ha as delicious?

In 1898 several companies merged to becom tional Biscuit Company. That company is now Nabisco Foods Group, and it still makes Fig N

Mayonnaise

It must have been one fun party! The year was 1756. The French army, under the Duke of Richelieu, had just defeated the British on the island of Minorca, off the coast of Spain.

Even the duke's chef honored the victory with some great food for the celebration, including a special new dressing. He called it *mahonnaise,* after the island's port city, which was named Mahón. Later the name was changed to mayonnaise.

The Nutmeg State

Most of the states in the United States have nicknames. New Jersey is the Garden State. Georgia is the Peach State. Utah is the Beehive State.

But why is Connecticut called the Nutmeg State? Nutmeg is not grown there. Residents don't consume record amounts of nutmeg. The state is not shaped like a nutmeg.

Nutmeg is a valuable spice, and many years ago unscrupulous traders from Connecticut made counterfeit nutmegs out of wood and sold them as the real thing. Thus the state earned its nickname.

Today the residents are amused by their history and sell wooden nutmegs as souvenirs.

Sardines

Why can't you buy fresh sardines at the grocery store?

The answer is surprising: because a sardine is not a sardine until it is packed in a sardine can.

Actually, there is no living fish called a sardine. Any one of twenty different species might end up as a canned sardine. The most common are young herring and pilchard.

The name sardine comes from the island of Sardinia, where sardines were first canned in 1834.

Turkey

Four hundred years ago the African guinea fowl found its way onto English dinner plates. This tasty bird had originated in Africa, but it had been imported to Turkey before being introduced in western Europe. Since it had come to England from Turkey, the English called it the turkey-cock.

When the English came to North America, they saw a native bird and assumed it was the same guinea fowl they were already familiar with, the turkey-cock. So they called the American bird a turkey.

Later it was discovered that this American bird was *not* the same species, but by then everyone recognized it by the name *turkey.* (Surprisingly, the natives called it a *furkee.*)

So the American bird retained the name of a country it had never even visited. And today Thanksgiving would hardly be Thanksgiving without the un-Turkish turkey.

FUN FACTS ABOUT TURKEY

Each Thanksgiving Day, Americans consume an average of 736 million pounds of turkey.

While many people get tired after eating on Thanksgiving Day, the tryptophan in turkey doesn't really take effect because of all the other amino acids present. Rather, the unusually large, carbohydrate-rich meal most people eat is more likely the culprit.

Turkey is healthy, as it's rich in zinc and vitamin B3, both of which are good for your eyes.

Mature turkeys have on average 3,500 feathers!

FOOD FOR THOUGHT

TWELVE MONTHS OF FOOD FESTS

Every American city, town, and village finds a reason to celebrate, and those events include food. Watch your local newspaper for the nearest festival. If you're traveling, ask a librarian for a book on festivals, or consult *Chase's Calendar of Events.*

Here's a year's sample of celebrations with mighty appetizing names!

- In January the community of Holtville, California, the "Home of the Carrot," hosts the Holtville Carrot Festival.
- February is the month of California Kiwifruit Day, and of the annual Pancake Race between Olney, England, and Liberal, Kansas.
- In Hermann, Missouri, otherwise known as the "Sausage Capital of Missouri," a Wurstfest is held each March.
- Take your pick in April of the Ham and Yam Festival (in Smithfield, North Carolina), the Spinach Festival (in Alma, Arkansas), and the World Grits Festival (in St. George, South Carolina).
- Residents of Springfield, Massachusetts, serve the world's largest pancake breakfast during the month of May.

- In June, during their strawberry festival, the people of Lebanon, Oregon, make the world's largest strawberry shortcake. Meanwhile, the Luling, Texas, community hosts its annual Watermelon Thump.
- New York's Coney Island hot-dog-eating contest is a July highlight, as are the baking of the world's largest cherry pie in George, Washington, and the sidewalk egg-frying contest in Oatman, Arizona.
- August is a savory month, from the Mushroom Festival in Telluride, Colorado, to the Rutabaga Festival in Askov, Minnesota.
- Don't miss Okrafest!, held in Checotah, Oklahoma, each September, the same month that Shelley, Idaho, hosts the Idaho Potato Harvest Festival.
- Once October comes around, it's time for the Big Pig Jig in Vienna, Georgia, the Whole Enchilada Fiesta in Las Cruces, New Mexico, and the Circleville, Ohio, Pumpkin Show, the "Greatest Free Show on Earth."
- November's the month of the Chitlin Strut, held in Salley, South Carolina, the "World Chitlin Capital."
- And to finish the year in style, Berrien Springs, Michigan, throws its annual Christmas Pickle Festival.

CHAPTER 3

FOUR-LEGGED FOOD

What are horses and puppies doing on the menu? Never fear: Some of the four-legged foods in this chapter aren't what they seem. Their histories might surprise you.

Hamburger and Steak Tartare

Almost everyone has asked at one time, "Why is it called hamburger if there's no ham in it?"

The hamburger's history goes back to medieval times, when tribes roamed the Russian steppes. Known as the Tatars, these tribes would steal cattle, shred the meat, and eat it raw.

As the Tatars traveled, they introduced their food to others. Along the way, salt, pepper, and onion juice were added to the shredded raw meat. This dish became known as steak tartare.

The Tatars traded with the Germans, and they introduced the shredded-meat dish to the inhabitants of the German port of Hamburg. Often the Germans ate the meat raw, as the Tatars had eaten it. But sometimes they cooked it. Soon the cooked version became known as the Hamburg steak.

Some say the Hamburg steak came to America with German immigrants in the 1880s. Since these immigrants were from Hamburg, they were known as Hamburgers, and soon the Hamburg steak also became known as a hamburger.

Three towns in America claim that the hamburger-as-a-sandwich was first made there: Athens, Texas; Hamburg, New York; and Seymour, Wisconsin. But most sources say the hamburger (in a bun) became popular after it was introduced at the St. Louis World's Fair in 1904.

FUN FACTS ABOUT HAMBURGERS

The largest hamburger ever made weighed just over a ton and was 10 feet in diameter.

Approximately 50 billion burgers are consumed in the United States each year, with the average American eating a burger three times a week.

Almost 60 percent of all sandwiches sold worldwide are hamburgers.

There is a Hamburger Hall of Fame in Seymour, Wisconsin.

One of the most expensive burgers available in the United States costs $5,000.

During World War I, hamburgers were sometimes called Liberty Sandwiches.

Horseradish

Horseradish is a member of the mustard family. Its root looks like a radish. When the root is grated, it makes a very spicy condiment that is used to flavor dishes or as a spread on sandwiches.

Horseradish is *not* something horses like. In fact, the "horse" in horseradish does not have anything to do with the four-legged animal. There are two theories on its origin.

The first says *horse* is a misspelling and mispronunciation of the word *coarse*. The same meaning of "coarse" or "rough" is used in the names of other plants, such as horse balm, horsemint, horseplum, horse chestnut, and horsebean. It is also used in *horseplay* and *horse laugh*.

The second theory says the plant was called *meerrettich* in German, which means "sea radish," since one variety of the plant grows by the sea. The English mispronounced the German word as "mareradish." Since a mare is a female horse, the word then became *horseradish*.

Hot Dog

The sausage now known as the hot dog started out with the name frankfurter or wiener (short for wienerwurst). Two different European cities claim to be the birthplace of this sausage. In 1987 Frankfurt-am-Main, Germany, celebrated the 500th birthday of the frankfurter. But Vienna (Wien), Austria, claims that wieners originated *there.*

In 1880 an American named Antoine Feuchtwanger was a sausage vendor in St. Louis. He loaned gloves to his customers to wear so that they would not burn their fingers while eating the hot food. But people walked away with the gloves, thus cutting into his profits.

So Mr. Feuchtwanger replaced the gloves with a sliced bread roll. The hot dog was invented!

It didn't get its name until 1903. T. A. "Tad" Dorgan, a sports cartoonist, was attending a baseball game at New York City's Polo Grounds. He heard the vendors calling, "Get your red hots! Get your dachshund sausages while they're red hot!" Dorgan drew a cartoon of a dachshund inside a bun. But he didn't know how to spell *dachshund.* So beneath the cartoon he wrote "hot dog."

Hush Puppies

Hush puppies are little fried corn cakes made by dropping corn batter into hot grease.

There's a legend about the name: A group of Southerners

were out hunting, and they had their hounds with them. One evening the hunters were frying catfish over the campfire. The hounds were hungry, and when they smelled the catfish cooking, they began whimpering and begging.

One of the hunters rolled up some balls of cornmeal batter and dropped them into the pot to fry with the fish. When the fried balls were golden brown, he tossed them to the dogs with the command "Hush, puppies!"

The dogs ate the fried batter and stopped whimpering. So the cook tried one of the hush puppies. It was delicious, and a Southern delicacy was born.

HUSH PUPPIES

Recipe

2 eggs, beaten
1/2 cup white sugar
1 large onion, diced
1 cup self-rising flour
1 cup self-rising cornmeal
1 quart oil (for frying)

In a bowl, mix together the eggs, sugar, and onion. Gradually blend in the flour and cornmeal. Set the batter aside and heat 2 inches of oil to 365°F. Drop batter in rounded teaspoonfuls carefully into the hot oil, and fry until golden brown. Remove from heat and drain them of oil briefly on paper towels. To maintain the oil temperature, cook in small batches.

Makes 8 servings.

Sirloin

There is a great story about how the sirloin cut of beef got its name. King Henry VIII (or perhaps it was King James I, or perhaps King Charles II) of England was served an unusually good piece of meat. It was so good, the king decided it deserved to be made a knight. Drawing his sword, the king tapped the steak and said, "I dub thee Sir Loin."

Etymologists insist the story is not true. They say *sirloin* was originally spelled *surloin* and comes from the French *surlonge,* which means "above the loin." The sirloin is cut from the hindquarters just above the loin of the animal.

FOOD FOR THOUGHT

FOUR AND TWENTY BLACKBIRDS

Sing a song of sixpence,
A pocket full of rye;
Four and twenty blackbirds
Baked in a pie.
When the pie was opened,
The birds began to sing;
Wasn't that a dainty dish
To set before the king?

You know it as a silly nursery rhyme, but it's more than that. It's true!

In the Middle Ages in Europe, banquets were elaborate and extravagant affairs. Outlandish ideas amazed and delighted the guests at these dinners.

A pre-Renaissance recipe has recently been found for a huge pie. When the pie was cut, live rabbits, birds, frogs, or other small animals would pop out. Sometimes even dwarves were hidden inside the pie. The dwarves would emerge, walk down the length of the table, and sing, recite poetry, or do tricks to entertain the guests.

One source says the "four and twenty blackbirds" in this rhyme refer to French musicians baked in a pie in 1454 during the Feast of the Pheasant for the Duke of Burgundy. When the pie was cut open, the musicians, who were dressed in black, played.

CHAPTER 4

EAT, DRINK, AND BE MERRY

This chapter is not the favorite of nutritionists.
The foods here aren't necessarily
healthy, but they sure are fun!
The party starts now.

Canapé

People who go to fancy parties eat canapés.

A canapé is a small piece of bread or cracker topped with something yummy. It's usually served before a meal. Surprisingly, the word originally came from the Greek *konops*, which means "mosquito." When the Greeks hung a curtain around their couch for protection against the mosquitoes, it was called a *konopion*. The Latin version, *canopeum*, came to mean simply a bed or couch. In French, the word became *canapé* and meant a couch or little seat.

Whoever named the tasty tidbit a canapé must have thought of the cracker as a little seat for something delicious.

Chess Pie

Chess pie is made without fruit. Its filling is sugar, cream, and eggs, baked in a crust.

Pie was once stored in a pie safe or a pie chest, a piece of furniture about four feet tall with shelves the right size to slide a pie into. A door on the pie chest kept mice and flies away. Some say that since this particular pie kept well in pie chests, it became known as chest pie, then chess pie.

A more amusing story says that a visitor to the South went into a restaurant. The waitress told him that a piece of pie was included with the meal.

The diner was delighted and ordered apple pie.

"No apple pie," the waitress said.

"Then I'll have cherry pie," said the diner.

"No cherry pie, either," said the waitress.

"Well, what kind of pie do you have?" he asked.

"Jes' pie."

So the sugar-cream-and-egg pie became known as chess pie.

CHESS PIE

Recipe

1/2 cup butter, softened
2 cups white sugar
1 teaspoon vanilla extract
4 eggs
1 tablespoon cornmeal
1/4 cup evaporated milk
1 tablespoon distilled white vinegar
1 9-inch unbaked pie shell

Preheat the oven to 425°F. In a bowl, mix together the butter, sugar, and vanilla. Add the eggs and stir until mixed. Mix in the cornmeal, evaporated milk, and vinegar until the batter is completely smooth. Once the oven is preheated, bake for 10 minutes before reducing heat to 300°F and baking for another 40 minutes. Let the pie cool before serving.

Makes 1 pie.

Hors d'Oeuvre

The term *hors d'oeuvre* is often found on menus in the United States. But how many people know what it really means?

The literal interpretation is "outside the main work." This French phrase was originally used by architects. It referred to an outbuilding—a building not included in the architect's primary design.

Chefs then borrowed the term to label a food not usually served with dinner. It entered the English language in the early 1700s. Literally, it now means something served outside (usually before) the main meal.

Lollipop

Which of these two theories do you believe?

The first says *lolly* is an English word for tongue, and *pop* is the noise made when sucking on the candy, not to mention the fact that one pops it into the mouth. The English had a hard candy called a lollipop, but theirs was not on a stick.

Here's the second theory. In the early 1900s a Connecticut candymaker, George Smith, put the candy on a stick and named it the lollipop in honor of a famous racehorse of the day named Lolly Pop.

Since most Americans called this candy on a stick

a sucker, the term *lollipop* might have faded from use. But in 1934 a six-year-old actress named Shirley Temple appeared in the movie *Bright Eyes.* In one famous scene, she sang the song "On the Good Ship Lollipop." That song ensured the popularity of the term we still use today.

Pie

Homemakers in the 1300s didn't want to waste any food, so they often put leftovers (such as meat, potatoes, and vegetables) together in a pastry crust.

In those years the bird we call the magpie was simply referred to as a pie. The thieving pie made a nest with things like sticks, string, and chicken feathers. Anything the bird could find went into the nest.

The dish of leftovers in a crust was made the same way and looked like the pie's nest. So the dish was called a pie.

Pretzel

Wouldn't you think that history would have recorded the name of the person who came up with something as terrific as the pretzel? But that's not what happened. All we know is that in 610 CE a monk in northern Italy first twisted the pretzel into its unusual shape. When children learned their prayers, he rewarded them with the bread shaped to represent the folded arms of children in prayer.

The word *pretzel* comes either from the Latin *pretiole,* which means "little gift," or from the Italian *bracciatelli,* which means "small arms."

FUN FACTS ABOUT PRETZELS

The largest pretzel in the world weighed 1,728 pounds!

April 26 is National Pretzel Day.

Pretzels without salt are called "baldies" because they lack any toppings.

The average American eats 2 pounds of pretzels each year.

Sundae

Soda fountains were very popular in the late 1800s. One favorite treat was the ice cream soda. It was made with scoops of ice cream and flavored soda water.

But religious leaders considered "sucking sodas" to be vulgar. Further, some people thought that anything so delicious must be sinful. So sodas could not be sold on Sunday, the holy day of the week.

Ice cream merchants came up with the idea of serving ice cream and syrup *without* the soda water. It was something people could enjoy on Sunday, so it was called a Sunday. Out of respect for the Lord's day, the spelling was changed to *sundae*.

Three cities claim to have originated the ice cream sundae. In Evanston, Illinois, they say the sundae was first made by William Garwood at Garwood's Drug Store. Unfortunately, no date is available.

In Two Rivers, Wisconsin, they claim the sundae was made in 1896 at an ice cream parlor operated by E. C. Berners.

An Ithaca, New York, newspaper dated April 11, 1892, advertises a "cherry Sunday."

No matter where the sundae was first concocted, we're glad someone thought up the idea.

FOOD FOR THOUGHT

GREAT MOMENTS IN CANDY HISTORY

In 1765 the first United States chocolate factory began production in Massachusetts. In 1847 Oliver Chase invented and patented the first American candy-making machine. But it wasn't until the price of sugar fell at the end of the nineteenth century that people were able to experiment with and produce affordable candy.

Here are some favorite candies and the dates they were introduced:

1894 Hershey's chocolate bar

1896 Tootsie Roll

1901 Necco candy wafers

1907 Hershey's Kisses

1912 Goo Goo clusters

1912 Life Savers

1917 Clark bar

1920 Baby Ruth

1921 Oh Henry!

1922 Charleston Chew

1922 Mounds

1923 Butterfinger

1923 Milky Way

1923 Reese's peanut butter cups

1924 Bit-O-Honey

1925 Mr. Goodbar

1926 Milk Duds

1928 Heath bar

1930 Snickers

1932 Three Musketeers

1941 M&M's (plain)

1947 Almond Joy

1949 Junior Mints

1954 M&M's (peanut)

CHAPTER 5

WHAT'S IN THAT SHOPPING CART?

What's in a typical grocery shopping cart? A little of this, a little of that—an interesting assortment of odds and ends. Here's a random yet amusing sample of foods with fascinating histories of how their names came to be.

Bread and Butter Pickles

Dill pickles are flavored with dill. Sweet pickles are sweetened with sugar. Watermelon pickles are made from watermelon rind. So, are bread and butter pickles made from bread and butter?

Actually, no.

Sometime around 1900, a homemaker (some say her name was Mrs. Fanning) made jars and jars of sweet pickles using her own special recipe. She had more than her family could eat, so she opened a roadside stand and sold her pickles to passersby. She called them bread and butter pickles, since the money she earned provided the family with bread and butter, as well as other necessities.

FUN FACTS ABOUT PICKLES

Shakespeare coined the phrase "in a pickle" in his play *The Tempest*.

November 14 is National Pickle Day.

The average American consumes 9 pounds of pickles a year.

Pickles are made in at least 60 percent of U.S. states, with Michigan and North Carolina making the most.

A U.S. Supreme Court ruling established that cucumbers, which some pickles are made from, are technically a fruit of the vine. However, they are usually known as a vegetable.

Coconut

The coconut is the fruit of the coconut palm tree. It resembles a human head and has thin fibers that look like dry human hair. At the base of the coconut fruit, three indentations make the coconut look like a face with two eyes and a mouth.

In the 1400s explorers from Portugal discovered the fruit growing on islands in the South Pacific and Indian Oceans. They decided the indentations looked like a *coco,* which meant "grinning face." They called the fruit a coconut.

Eggplant

What strange connotations the eggplant has inspired! A Lebanese eggplant recipe is called *baba ganoush,* which means "spoiled old daddy." Eggplant is also one of the ingredients in a Turkish recipe called *imam bayaldi.* Translated, this means "the priest has fainted."

Eggplants originated in India and were introduced to Spain in the twelfth century by the Arabs. Before the fifteenth century, the vegetable was used only for decoration, as people believed it was poisonous. In Italy, where eggplant was suspected of causing insanity, it was called *mala insana,* "mad apple." Later, when people had begun eating the vegetable, Europeans called it the "apple of love," for it was believed to arouse passion.

From apples we move to eggs. Why do we now call this large purple vegetable an eggplant?

As with most vegetables, there are different types of eggplant. The edible part of one variety is small and white. It was named eggplant since it looked like an egg. Once the name was established in the middle 1700s, it was also applied to the purple variety.

Marmalade

Marmalade is a kind of thick jam. Today most American marmalades are made from oranges. Here's a great legend about its name.

Mary, Queen of Scots, ruled Scotland in the sixteenth century. Mary often felt ill and would not eat. Her French-speaking servants would say *"Marie est malade,"* which means "Mary is ill." The only thing they could get her to eat was a sweet made of oranges and honey. *Marie est malade* became *Marie malade* (sick Mary), and her favorite food soon was known as *mar-malade.*

Unfortunately, etymologists say the story is not true. They say the word was handed from one language to another. The original Greek *melimelon* meant "sweet apple." The Romans changed it to *melemelum.* Then the Portuguese used the word *marmelo* for the quince. Since they made marmalade from quinces, the jam was called *marmelada.* And the French changed it to *marmalade.*

By the time it got into the English language, it meant a jam made of oranges. *Marmalade* has been in the English language since the early 1500s. But Mary, Queen of Scots, was not even born until 1542. So much for great legends!

Po' Boy

If there were a prize for the number of names for the same sandwich, the po' boy would probably win. It has been called a hoagie, a grinder, a hero, a submarine, and a torpedo, among others.

The sandwich is a small loaf of French bread sliced from end to end. It's filled with meats, cheeses, dressings, vegetables, and relishes.

Some say the name po' boy, or "poor boy," came

about because the sandwich has all the ingredients of a full meal, yet the price is affordable even for someone who's poor.

But there is a more widely accepted story for the origin of the term. During a streetcar workers' strike in New Orleans in 1929, a sandwich shop called Martin Brothers offered free food to any "poor boy," or union member. After the strike was settled, Benny and Clovis Martin, the owners of the shop, posted a sign that read, "Originators of 'Poor Boy Sandwiches.'"

The term *grinder* is used more often in New England. The name might derive from the ground beef used in the meatball versions of the sandwich. Others say it's because the food requires so much chewing. *Grinders* is a slang term for teeth.

The term *hoagie* originated around Philadelphia or in New Jersey. One source says the name was inspired by the hokey-pokey, which was an inexpensive ice cream. Another says *hoagie* was originally *hoggie,* since a person would have to be a hog to eat the entire sandwich.

The names *submarine* and *torpedo* refer to the shape of the sandwich. It is thought these terms originated either in Pittsburgh or near a navy base in Groton, Connecticut.

The term *hero* is used in the New York City area and northern New Jersey, because it supposedly takes a hero-sized appetite to eat the whole sandwich.

Pumpernickel

There's a legend that pumpernickel bread got its name from Napoleon. When he was in Germany, he tasted it but didn't like it, so he fed it to his horse, Nicol. He said jeeringly, *"C'est du pain pour Nicol!"*—"It's bread for Nicol!"

Pain pour Nicol quickly became *pumpernickel*.

It's a great story, but it can't be true. People were already calling the bread pumpernickel in 1756, and Napoleon wasn't born until 1769.

The real story is even better: The German word *pumpern* means "flatulence." *Nickel* comes from the name of a goblin or devil. So *pumpernickel* actually means "devil's fart"—the effect the bread has on some people's digestive systems.

FOOD FOR THOUGHT

PHONY BALONEY

Warning: Things aren't always what they seem. Think twice before you order new foods from a menu. Do prairie strawberries sound like the perfect summer dessert? They are actually beans, nicknamed by cowboys who longed for variety as they worked on the dry plains of the American West. Similarly, the people who lived along the south shore of Massachusetts got tired of always eating codfish. So they gave it a new name: Cape Cod turkey.

Here are some other surprising food "fakes":

- *Black-eyed peas* are named for the black spot at one side of the seed. But black-eyed peas are not peas. They're beans.

- *Bombay duck* is not a duck. It's not even a bird. It's a fish called the bummalo, which is dried and eaten in curries.

- *Head cheese* isn't cheese. It's a lunch meat made from the head and feet and sometimes the heart and tongue of a pig. This meat is boiled for hours, then poured into a cheese-shaped mold and chilled until the gelatin sets.

- A *peanut* is not a pea and it's not a nut. It's a legume—a bean. It is also known by the name *goober,* which is a mispronunciation and a misspelling of the African word *nguba.*

- *Welsh rabbit* is not made with rabbit. It is actually cheese melted with butter, milk, and Worcestershire sauce and spread on buttered toast. The name originated in Shakespeare's time as a humorous jab at the Welsh, who were considered so poor they couldn't even afford rabbit meat.

- *Wild rice* is not really rice. It is the seeds of a water grass found in rivers and lakes.

CHAPTER 6

TALKING TURKEY

Friends usually get along like two peas in a pod,
making life a bowl of cherries. They're as sweet as
honey and act nuttier than a fruitcake. Then one
goes bananas and drops the other like a hot potato.
They both walk on eggshells and act as cool as a
cucumber as long as one has a bone to pick. But
once they sit down to chew the fat or talk turkey,
things are keen as mustard once again.
Food is always on the tip of our tongue. But what
are the origins of our favorite terms and sayings?

Baker's Dozen

Meaning: Thirteen

In England in the thirteenth century, bakers had a
bad reputation for selling underweight bread. Strict laws
were passed in 1266 with heavy penalties if the weight
of a baker's bread was insufficient. But using the equipment available at the time, it was difficult to make all
the loaves the same size. So bakers began giving an extra
loaf of bread with every dozen (twelve) loaves a person
bought. Thirteen then became known as a baker's dozen.

Bring Home the Bacon

Meaning: To earn the money that supports the household

This phrase might have originated in the year 1111 with a noblewoman who went by the name Juga, or it might have started in 1244 with Lord Robert de Fitzwalter. One of these British nobles announced that a side of bacon would be given to any married person who would travel to Dunmow (in Essex County, England), kneel on two stones at the church door, and swear that for at least a year and a day there had been no fighting in the marriage and no wish to be unmarried.

A side of bacon was a great reward, but in the 528 years the prize was offered, only eight couples could claim it.

A second theory on the origin of this phrase says that there was a sport at early American county fairs that involved trying to catch a greased pig. If a person could catch the pig, he could take it home as a prize. Since bacon is made from pigs, the saying "bring home the bacon" referred to winning the prize pig.

FUN FACTS ABOUT BACON

Bacon has some health benefits, as it contains vitamin B3, which is known to promote good brain function.

Our love for bacon dates back to the sixteenth century BCE when the Chinese began salting pork bellies.

The BLT, or bacon, lettuce, and tomato sandwich, became popular during World War II.

September 3 is International Bacon Day.

Corny

Meaning: Unsophisticated, old-fashioned, or excessively sentimental

One story says this expression was first used in the 1890s. Companies selling seeds sent their catalogs to farmers. Jokes and riddles were added to the seed catalogs, but the jokes were obvious and trite. They became known as corn catalog jokes, then corn jokes, and eventually the adjective *corny* was born.

Another story is that when traveling vaudeville shows performed in the Corn Belt of the midwestern United States, the naive audiences liked old-fashioned, simple humor. The comedians called it corn-fed humor, since their audiences ate a lot of corn. By the 1930s *corny* had become part of America's vocabulary.

Couch Potato

Meaning: A person who spends a lot of time watching television

Most phrases come into the language gradually and cannot be attributed to a specific time or person. "Couch potato" is an exception. Tom Iacino, a man from California, coined the term in 1976. "Couch Potato" was then trademarked. A club was formed, a newsletter was published, and merchandise (such as T-shirts and dolls) was sold.

TYPES OF POTATOES

- Blue or purple potato
- Fingerling potato
- Petite potato
- Russet potato
- Red potato
- White potato
- Yellow potato

Within the seven categories above, there are more than two hundred varieties of potatoes sold throughout the United States!

Eat Humble Pie

Meaning: To suffer humiliation, or to admit a mistake

In the Middle Ages, the English lord of a manor and his guests would feast on fresh venison after a successful hunt. But the "numbles" (sometimes called "umbles") were for the servants. Numbles were the liver, heart, tongue, brain, kidneys, and intestines.

The servants often made the numbles into a pie with other things such as vegetables. This was called a numble pie. Because it was a poor man's dish—a meal for the humble—the name soon changed to humble pie.

The words *humble* and *humiliate* both derive from the same Latin word *humilis,* meaning "lowly." So today when we "eat humble pie," we are enduring humiliation by apologizing, "eating our words."

Give the Cold Shoulder

Meaning: To snub someone; act unfriendly and distant

During the Middle Ages in Europe, when a welcome visitor arrived, the host served a hot meal, including the best cut of roasted meat. The undesirable, leftover meat was given to the servants and the dogs.

However, when a visitor stayed too long, the host would hint that the guest had worn out his welcome by serving a shoulder cut of unheated meat. The guest was literally given the cold shoulder!

Sell Like Hotcakes

Meaning: To sell well and quickly

Hotcakes are the same as pancakes, griddle cakes, or flapjacks. Beginning in the 1600s hotcakes were sold at fairs, carnivals, and other festive events. They became the bestselling snack at these celebrations. (Even today pancake breakfasts are great fund-raisers.)

By the nineteenth century the term had come into

general use in the language, and any popular purchase was said to be selling like hotcakes.

Spill the Beans

Meaning: To divulge a secret

Many ancient Greeks belonged to secret societies or clubs. They were very strict about who joined their organizations, and they voted on new members. The voting was done by walking past an opaque jar and secretly dropping either a white bean or a black bean inside. A white bean meant the voter was in favor of admitting the applicant, and a black bean meant the voter was opposed.

Only the top officers in the organization were allowed to know how many black beans had been dropped in the jar to reject a new member. But sometimes someone would accidentally knock over the jar and "spill the beans"—letting the secret out.

Top Banana

Meaning: The person in charge

Early in the twentieth century a popular vaudeville or burlesque act involved the sharing of bananas. The star was called the "top banana."

The phrase became popular, and the leading star in any show soon became known as the top banana. Today the phrase can be used in any field from sports to business, as well as entertainment.

Your Goose Is Cooked

Meaning: You're really in trouble now

One story says that in 1560 the residents of a town were being attacked by Mad King Eric XIV of Sweden. The townsfolk hung a goose from a tower; it was their way of saying they thought their attackers were as stupid as geese.

Of course, this made the king mad. So he set fire to the town and "cooked their goose."

Another story claims that the saying comes from the old fable about the goose that laid the golden egg. The peasant couple who owned the goose were impatient to get rich. They didn't want to wait for the goose to lay its golden eggs. So they killed the goose to get at the eggs inside. But the eggs inside the goose had not yet turned to gold, and now they had killed any hope of future golden eggs. They were no richer, probably hungry, and most likely they cooked their goose.

Etymologists say the source of the saying dates to 1851. There were religious conflicts in England at the time, and when two religious leaders made plans for a visit, a street ballad was sung that included the line "If they come here, we'll cook their goose."

FOOD FOR THOUGHT

PUT YOUR MONEY WHERE YOUR MOUTH IS

Paper money didn't exist until about thirteen hundred years ago. Coins were the first money. In ancient Turkey, a type of coin was first issued around 650 BCE. But even after coins were invented, they were sometimes useless. A ship's captain with a coin from Rome could not spend it in India. So people still used the barter system, trading one item of universal value for another. Frequently these items were food.

- In ancient Egypt, payroll records indicate that people were paid in bread. Murals of royal bakeries have been found in tombs of Egyptian pharaohs—their way of showing the pharaoh's wealth.

- Since raisins don't spoil in hot weather, they were so highly valued in ancient Rome that you could trade two jars of raisins for one slave boy.

- In Japan the only primitive currency was rice. Most Japanese words expressing value are related to the word *rice.*

- Pepper was a highly valued spice in the Middle Ages. Taxes were paid with pepper in many European cities, and soldiers were rewarded for their victories with bonuses of pepper.

- In 408 CE Alaric the Hun demanded three thousand pounds of pepper to withdraw his troops from Rome. (Though the ransom was paid, he plundered the city anyway.)

- In the early 1400s dried fish was the medium of exchange in Iceland. One pair of black leather shoes was equal to four dried stockfish.

- Sugar became a principal West Indian medium of exchange in the 1600s. In Barbados fines were levied in pounds of sugar. If a master or a freedman cursed, he would be fined four pounds of sugar for each offense. Servants had to pay two pounds of sugar each time they cursed.

- On the Leeward Islands in 1668, a salary of fourteen thousand pounds of sugar was paid to "an able preaching Orthodox Minister." The minister charged a hundred pounds of sugar to perform marriage ceremonies.

- Tea was used as money for nine hundred years, through the nineteenth century in China and other parts of Asia. Packed hard and formed into bricks, tea served as currency in Tibet, Mongolia, and some parts of Siberia. Even in the late 1800s in Mongolia, a sheep was worth

12 to 15 bricks of tea, and a camel was worth 120 to 150 bricks.

- In 1922 the Austrian Medical Association set doctors' fees on the "butter standard." A consultation cost one pound of butter.

- Coconuts have been used as recently as one hundred years ago on the island of Yap, near Guam. Two coconuts would buy one match; ten coconuts a bread roll; forty coconuts a twelve-ounce bottle of gasoline; twenty thousand coconuts a cooking stove. And on the island of Faraulip, in the South Pacific, a small boat could be purchased for three hundred coconuts.

- Even in the first half of the twentieth century, food was used as currency. Eggs were accepted as payment in the South Pacific, Guatemala, and Scotland. In Vienna, farmers paid for doctors' services in flour. And the tribes of northern Siberia bartered jam.

CHAPTER 7

BY WORD OF MOUTH

Food is such a constant part of our lives that it has even sneaked into our language through words that now don't seem to have anything to do with food or eating. Surprise! Look into the histories of these familiar words and you'll find food hidden in all of them.

Carnival

The word *carnival* began from the Latin words *carne,* meaning "meat," and *vale,* meaning "farewell," and it refers to a time when Christians consumed a lot of meat before beginning Lent, a six-week period of abstinence that occurred before Easter. The day before Lent was called *carne vale*—"farewell to meat." In the 1600s *carnival* began to be used as a term for any festive time.

POPULAR CARNIVAL
FOODS

- Corn dogs
- Corn on the cob
- Cotton candy
- Elephant ears
(made of dough, not elephants!)
- Fried pickles
- Funnel cake

Company and Companion

A companion is a person who spends time with another.

A company is a group of people who work together.

Both of these words come from the Latin *com*, which means "with" or "together," and *panis*, which means "bread." Whether it is with your companion or the people in your company, these words actually mean to share bread.

(And it's true that companies have the goal of sharing bread—*bread* being another word for money!)

Form

Webster's New World Dictionary defines "form" as a "shape, outline, or configuration." When dressmakers make clothing, they use a human-shaped form. When concrete is poured for a building or a sidewalk, the metal or boards into which it is poured are called forms.

The word *form* is actually taken from the French and Italian words for cheese: *formaggio* in Italian, *fromage* in

French. Both of these words come from a Greek term that meant not the cheese itself, but the shape of the basket in which the cheese was molded. We now use *form* to mean the shape of something.

Garbled

Four hundred years ago spices were transported to Europe and Africa from the East. When ships carrying herbs and spices arrived in Alexandria, in Egypt, the cargo was always damaged from the sea water, mildew, and rot, and it included a lot of sticks, stems, and other unusable parts of the plant.

The Arabic word *gharbala* meant to sift, sort out, or select the usable parts of the spice shipment. This term was also used with grain—meaning to remove the unwanted parts. The Italian word was *garbellare,* and from that we get the English word *garble.* When people separated the usable parts of something from those to be thrown away, they "garbled" it.

Garble was later used to mean the distorting or twisting of information to change its sense. Today the word *garble* has nothing to do with spices or grain, or with sifting out the waste from a shipment. Garbling now means creating a confused mess, or mixing up something, especially a story or radio transmission.

Lord and Lady

About 1,400 years ago in Anglo-Saxon England, food was scarce. Bread was a necessity. The head of the household guarded the bread supply. He was known as the *hlafweard,* with *hlaf* meaning "loaf" or "bread" and *weard* meaning "ward" or "keeper." *Hlafweard* later became *hlaford,* then *lord.*

At the same time, the lord's wife, as mistress of the house, had the privilege of making the bread. She was the *hlaefdige,* the "bread kneader." (*Dige* meant "to knead.") The word was later *ladah,* then *lady.*

FUN FACTS ABOUT BREAD

The average American consumes
53 pounds of bread each year.

The "pocket" in pita bread is made by
steam, which puffs up the dough as it
bakes and leaves a trapped bubble of air
when it cools and flattens.

Bread is a symbol of welcome in Russia.

In some places it is thought to be bad
luck to turn a loaf of bread upside down
or cut an unbaked loaf.

Parasite

Today the term *parasite* means a person, plant, or animal that lives at the expense of another without providing any benefit. We think of a tick, a leech, or a tapeworm as a parasite.

In ancient Greece, *parasitos* were guests at a meal. *Para* was Greek for "beside," and *sitos* meant "food." *Parasitos* literally meant "feeding beside" or "one who sits near food."

The *parasitos*—priests, war heroes, and government officials—were often welcome in the homes of wealthy hosts. But by the fourth century BCE, *parasitos* had begun taking advantage of their hosts and abusing their hospitality. As many of the guests enjoyed the wonderful food and gave only compliments in return, the word came to refer to people who lived at someone else's expense.

Precocious

The early Latin words *prae coquere* meant "to cook beforehand" or "to cook something before it was fully ripened." Later a word derived from it, *praecox,* referred to a fruit that ripened before its time.

Precocious now means that something is mature before it should be. It seldom refers to food, but instead to children who are overly sophisticated for their age.

Apricot is also derived from the same root word, as it is an early-ripening fruit.

Salary

Salad, salami, salary, salivate, salsa, salvation, sauce, and sausage: All of these words come from one common root. *Sal* is the Latin word for salt.

Salt is necessary to the human body. Without it, people would die. Today in the United States, salt is inexpensive and so frequently used in meals that health experts say Americans should reduce their consumption of it.

But more than two thousand years ago in ancient Rome, salt was scarce and very valuable. Besides a seasoning for food, it was also a preservative. Salt could make food last a long time in an age when there were no refrigerators or freezers.

Because salt was so valuable, Roman soldiers were paid a *salarium,* which was an allowance to buy salt. Later, *salarium* meant a soldier's pay. It is with that meaning that the word came into the English language as *salary.*

Union

Everyone knows that an onion is made of many layers that all fit tightly together to make one vegetable. The Latin word for "one" was *unus,* and the Latin for "onion" was *unio.* It is easy to see how *union* came to be applied to people who are joined together for a common cause—many becoming one.

FOOD FOR THOUGHT

A FORKFUL OF FORTUNE

One of the human being's first experiences—after hunger and thirst—was fear. What we didn't understand, we feared. And there was a *lot* that we didn't understand! People through the ages have looked to magicians, witch doctors, and fortune-tellers for help. They have believed that certain rituals, practices, or routines can ward off danger, calm angry gods, trick nasty spirits . . . or just plain bring good luck. And since food sustains life, many of the rituals have involved food. Today we call such beliefs superstitions. How many of these do you believe?

- When moving into a new home, carry in salt first to ensure wealth. If you next take in bread, you'll always be well fed.

- If you want to dream in color, eat three almonds before you go to sleep. For good dreams, eat chocolate at bedtime. And to avoid nightmares, be sure not to eat doughnuts right before going to bed.

- To keep vampires and other evil spirits away, hang garlic around your doors and windows.

- If you leave the top off a teapot, it means a stranger will soon visit.

- Eating bread crusts will make your hair curly.
- If you find a double yolk inside an egg, someone will soon marry.
- When two people break the turkey's wishbone, the person who ends up with the longest part will get her or his wish.
- Never stir a glass of milk with a fork. It will make the cow go dry.
- Bad luck will come to you if you let a slice of bread fall to the floor buttered side down.
- If two people reach for a saltshaker at the same time, they will soon quarrel.
- Do you want to dream of your future spouse? Sleep with a piece of wedding cake under your pillow.
- You can kill germs in a sickroom by hanging a peeled onion there or by placing half an onion on a windowsill. And to ward off disease, carry a red onion in your left pocket.
- It is bad luck to eat the last slice of bread on a plate. To prevent misfortune, toss the bread slice in the air before eating it.
- Your money will multiply if you rub your coins and bills with pomegranate seeds.

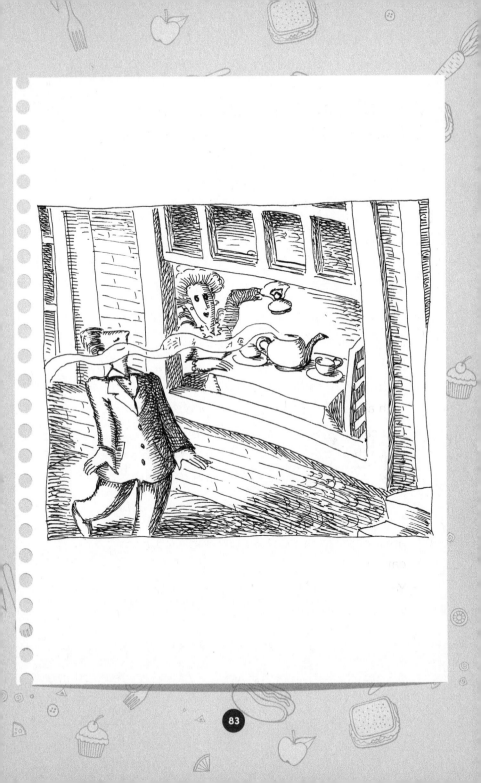

MEAL'S END

When dinner is finished, many people reach for a toothpick. How many? Enough so that Americans use thirty billion toothpicks a year.

Anthropologists believe that the toothpick was one of the first tools used by early humans. Fossil remains of early humans show grooves in the teeth, indicating that thirty-five thousand years ago our ancestors probably sat around the fire picking their teeth after a big hunt.

People have used toothpicks throughout history. Gold toothpicks in beautiful gold boxes have been found in Mesopotamian ruins dating to 3500 BCE.

Both the ancient Chinese and the ancient Romans carried "pocket sets" attached to their belts or hung around their necks. The pocket sets included a nail cleaner, tweezers, an ear scoop, and a toothpick. Until a hundred years ago, wealthy people had toothpicks that were often works of art. They carried them in special cases.

The first patent for a toothpick-manufacturing machine in the United States was issued in 1872 to Silas Noble and James P. Cooley of Massachusetts. Round toothpicks were introduced at the 1904 World's Fair in St. Louis.

Most of the toothpicks Americans use today are made in Strong, Maine, from birch trees. One tree produces four million toothpicks.

Selected Bibliography

American Heritage Cookbook and Illustrated History of American Eating and Drinking. New York: Simon and Schuster, 1964.

Ammer, Christine. *Fruitcakes and Couch Potatoes and Other Delicious Expressions.* New York: Penguin, 1995.

———. *Have a Nice Day—No Problem: A Dictionary of Clichés.* New York: Dutton, 1992.

Barnette, Martha. *Ladyfingers and Nun's Tummies: A Lighthearted Look at How Foods Got Their Names.* New York: Random House, 1997.

Brasch, R. *How Did It Begin? Customs and Superstitions and Their Romantic Origins.* New York: David McKay, 1965.

Brewer, E. Cobham. *Brewer's Dictionary of Phrase and Fable.* New York: Harper and Row, 1970.

Chase's Calendar of Events, 1998. Lincolnwood, Ill.: NTC/Contemporary, 1997.

Childers, Evelyn Jones. *Kiss a Mule, Cure a Cold: Omens, Signs and Sayings.* Atlanta: Peachtree, 1988.

Claiborne, Craig. *Craig Claiborne's The New York Times Food Encyclopedia.* New York: The New York Times Company, 1985.

Coyle, L. Patrick, Jr. *The World Encyclopedia of Food.* New York: Facts on File, 1982.

Einzig, Paul. *Primitive Money.* Oxford: Pergamon, 1966.

Freeman, Morton S. *The Story Behind the Word.* Philadelphia: ISI, 1985.

———. *Even-Steven and Fair and Square: More Stories Behind the Words.* New York: Plume, 1993.

"Fun Facts About Chicken Wings." Shooters Wood Fire Grill. May 17, 2016. shooterswoodfiregrill.com/blog/2016/05/fun-facts-about-chicken-wings.

Funk, Charles Earle. *A Hog on Ice and Other Curious Expressions.* New York: Harper and Row, 1948.

Funk, Charles Earle, and Charles Earle Funk, Jr. *Horsefeathers and Other Curious Words*. New York: Harper and Brothers, 1958.

Garrison, Webb B. *Why You Say It*. New York: Abingdon, 1955.

Hendrickson, Robert. *Facts on File Encyclopedia of Word and Phrase Origins*. New York: Facts on File, 1987.

Jacobs, Jay. *The Eaten Word: The Language of Food, the Food in Our Language*. New York: Carol, 1995.

Jones, Evan. *American Food: The Gastronomic Story*. Woodstock, N.Y.: Overlook, 1990.

Kim, Jenny. "9 Sizzlin' Facts About Bacon." aol.com. August 20, 2016. aol.com/article/2016/08/20/9-sizzlin-facts-about-bacon/21455183.

Lindsell-Roberts, Sheryl. *Loony Laws and Silly Statutes*. New York: Sterling, 1994.

Mariani, John F. *The Dictionary of American Food and Drink*. New Haven: Ticknor and Fields, 1983.

Morris, William, and Mary Morris. *Morris Dictionary of Word and Phrase Origins*. New York: Harper and Row, 1977.

Myrick, Richard. "Bread Fun Facts." Mobile-Cuisine.com. August 20, 2016. mobile-cuisine.com/did-you-know/bread-fun-facts.

——. "Fig Fun Facts." Mobile-Cuisine.com. August 20, 2016. mobile-cuisine.com/did-you-know/fig-fun-facts.

——. "Pickle Fun Facts." Mobile-Cuisine.com. August 20, 2016. mobile-cuisine.com/did-you-know/pickle-fun-facts.

Nuttle, Matthew. "9 Interesting Facts About Burgers for National Burger Day." News 9. August 27, 2015. news9.com/story/29893374/9-interesting-facts-about-burgers-for-national-burger-day.

Opie, Iona, and Moira Tatem (editors). *A Dictionary of Superstitions*. Oxford: Oxford University Press, 1989.

Oxford English Dictionary. 2nd ed. 20 vols. Oxford University Press, 1989. Continually updated at oed.com.

Panati, Charles. *Panati's Extraordinary Origins of Everyday Things*. New York: Harper and Row, 1987.

Pelton, Robert Wayne. *Laughable Laws and Courtroom Capers.* New York: Walker, 1993.

———. *Loony Laws . . . That You Never Knew You Were Breaking.* New York: Walker, 1990.

Seuling, Barbara. *It Is Illegal to Quack Like a Duck and Other Freaky Laws.* New York: Dutton, 1988.

"6 Facts About Pretzels That Will Make Your Mouth Water." The Global Franchise Group. September 17, 2015. pretzelmakerfranchise.com/blog/6-facts-about-pretzels-that-will-make-your-mouth-water.

Tannahill, Reay. *Food in History.* New York: Stein and Day, 1973.

Terban, Marvin. *Scholastic Dictionary of Idioms.* New York: Scholastic, 1996.

Trager, James. *The Food Chronology: A Food Lover's Compendium of Events and Anecdotes, from Prehistory to the Present.* New York: Henry Holt, 1995.

"Turkey History and Trivia." National Turkey Federation. eatturkey.com/why-turkey/history.

Index

A
almonds, 81
apricot, 79

B
baked Alaska, 16
baker's dozen, 59
baloney, 19
banana, 14
beef Stroganoff, 3
Big Apple, the, 18
black-eyed peas, 57
bologna, 14, 19
Bombay duck, 57
bread, 56, 69, 74, 78, 82
Buffalo wings, 20
butter, 71, 82

C
Caesar salad, 4
cake, 14, 82
canapé, 39
candy, 14, 47
cheese, 75
chess pie, 40
clam chowder, 14
coconut, 51, 71
cucumbers, 14

D
doughnuts, 81

E
eggplant, 52
eggs, 15, 71, 82
eggs Benedict, 5

F
festivals, 27
Fig Newtons, 21
fish
    dried, 70
    sardines, 24
flour, 71

G
garlic, 15, 81
graham crackers, 6
guinea fowl, 25

H
hamburger, 15, 30
head cheese, 57
hors d'oeuvre, 42
horseradish, 33
hot dog, 33
humble pie, 64
hush puppies, 34

I
ice cream, 15
    sundae, 45

J
jam, 71

L
laws, food-related, 14
lobster Newburg, 8
lollipop, 42

M
macadamia nuts, 9
marmalade, 53

WANT MORE UNUSUAL STORIES AND WEIRD, AMAZING FACTS?

Don't miss . . .

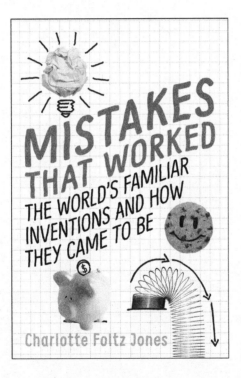

CHAPTER 1

· FAVORITE FOODS

Many cooks admit their favorite recipes were the result of accidents. But the numerous cases of food poisoning prove many food accidents don't work.

If you would like to experiment in the kitchen, a good book to start with is Vicki Cobb's *Science Experiments You Can Eat* (HarperCollins, New York). But be careful. The National Safety Council reports that almost eight hundred thousand victims of accidents involving home kitchen appliances and housewares are treated in hospital emergency rooms each year. So learn the safety rules and don't become a statistic.

KITCHEN SAFETY TIPS

✓ Ask permission from a parent or other adult before beginning any kitchen project.

✓ Always wash your hands before handling foods or cooking utensils.

✓ Read the recipe carefully and get out all ingredients and equipment before you begin.

✓ Follow the recipe exactly and measure accurately.

✓ Use electrical appliances only with an adult's supervision.

✓ When you are finished, put unused ingredients away and clean the kitchen. Never leave a mess.

Frozen Dinner Rolls

Baking rolls or bread from scratch is not quick.

The ingredients are mixed, then kneaded. The dough rises for up to two hours. Then it gets punched, divided into rolls, and baked for at least another hour.

Joe Gregor *knew* there must be an easier way for busy people to have hot rolls. He spent long hours trying to devise a method, but without success.

Then, one afternoon in 1949, Gregor was baking dinner rolls in his Avon Park, Florida, kitchen when the town's fire siren wailed. As a volunteer fireman, he had to respond to the fire. He quickly pulled his rolls from the oven and rushed out the door.

When he returned from the fire, Gregor examined the cold, half-cooked rolls. They were white and looked like plaster. Most people would have thrown the ugly mess in the garbage. But not Joe Gregor. He reheated his oven and finished cooking the rolls.

They were delicious! Gregor had accidentally discovered a method for making rolls ahead of time, yet serving them hot and fresh at the dinner table.

Gregor experimented to find the exact temperatures and times required for the first baking. He then revealed the directions to bakers everywhere.

Today, bakeries do the mixing, kneading, rising, and even part of the baking. Mr. or Ms. N. A. Hurry can buy frozen, partially cooked dinner rolls, heat them for ten minutes, and eat! . . . thanks to Joe Gregor and the Avon Park volunteer fire department.

Cheese

There he was: an ancient Arabian traveling across the desert with no one for company but a camel with yellow teeth, bad breath, and a bad temper.

At least the fellow had food along. He had poured some milk into a pouch made from a sheep's stomach. During his journey, he opened the pouch and discovered that the milk had separated and formed thick masses, which we call curd, and a watery fluid, which we call whey. The Arabian traveler had accidentally invented cheese.

Two elements had transformed milk into cheese: First, the sun had warmed the bag of milk during the journey. Second, the sheep-stomach bag contained dried digestive juices. The digestive juices included rennet, which is necessary to make cheese even today.

The Arabian traveler told his friends about his discovery, and for four thousand years, people have continued making cheese. Cheese quickly became important all over the world. Milk spoiled quickly, but by making cheese, people could preserve the milk's nutrition for long periods of time.

If you are an average American, you ate 33.7 pounds of cheese in 2013. That's what the National Cheese Institute estimates. According to the *International Dairy Federation,* while the United States is the largest producer of cheese, the average French person eats the most cheese—57 pounds each year.

Over two thousand varieties of cheese are produced around the world. If you tasted a different kind each week, it would take almost forty years to sample all the varieties. And by that time, someone would probably have developed some new ones to try, too.

FUN FACTS ABOUT CHEESE!

According to the *Guinness Book of World Records*, the largest cheese ever made was 40,060 pounds. It was made in 1988 in Wisconsin. A specially designed, refrigerated "cheese-mobile" moved the giant cheese from place to place.

The United States dairy industry sponsors National Dairy Month in June. It began as National Milk Month in 1937.

"Cheese" in other languages is:

French—*fromage*

Spanish—*queso*

Italian—*formaggio*

German—*Käse*

Polish—*ser*

Hungarian—*sajt*

Russian—*sir*

Japanese—*chiizu*

Swahili—*jibini*

Swedish—*ost*

Chocolate Chip Cookies

George Washington never tasted one.

Neither did Benjamin Franklin, Abraham Lincoln, or Mark Twain.

Unfortunately, they died before the chocolate chip cookie was invented.

Thanks to Ruth Wakefield, chocolate chip cookies were invented in 1938 and are available all over America today.

Wakefield did not plan to invent a cookie that would become the country's favorite. She was busy with the chores of running the Toll House Inn, located on the toll road between Boston and New Bedford, Massachusetts.

While mixing a batch of cookies, Wakefield discovered she was out of baker's chocolate. As a substitute, she broke some semisweet chocolate into small pieces and added them, intending to produce chocolate cookies.

When she removed the pan from the oven, Wakefield was surprised. The chocolate had not melted into the dough, and her cookies were not chocolate cookies. Wakefield had accidentally invented the chocolate chip cookie.

They were named Toll House Cookies after Ruth Wakefield's inn and are the most popular variety in America today. Estimates say seven billion chocolate chip cookies are consumed annually, and half the cookies baked in American homes are chocolate chip.

These popular treats have even provided full-time jobs; some vendors sell nothing but chocolate chip cookies.

They also made a political appearance in 1980. After Canadian diplomats assisted six American hostages to escape from Iran, the American people sent chocolate chip cookies to the Canadian embassy—our way of saying thanks.

If you would like to make chocolate chip cookies, the following recipe is furnished by Nestlé Foods for the original Toll House Cookies.

· Recipe ·

TOLL HOUSE COOKIES

- 2¼ cups unsifted flour
- 1 teaspoon baking soda
- 1 teaspoon salt
- 1 cup butter, softened
- ¾ cup white sugar
- ¾ cup firmly packed brown sugar
- 1 teaspoon vanilla extract
- 2 eggs
- 1 twelve-ounce package (2 cups) Nestlé Semi-Sweet Chocolate Morsels
- 1 cup chopped nuts

Preheat oven to 375° F. In small bowl, combine flour, baking soda, and salt; set aside. In large bowl, combine butter, white sugar, brown sugar, and vanilla extract; beat until creamy. Beat in eggs. Gradually add flour mixture, mixing well. Stir in chocolate morsels and nuts. Drop rounded teaspoonfuls of dough onto ungreased cookie sheets.

Bake for 8 to 10 minutes.

Makes 100 two-inch cookies.

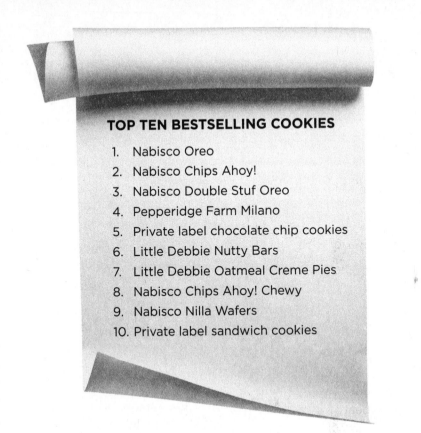

TOP TEN BESTSELLING COOKIES

1. Nabisco Oreo
2. Nabisco Chips Ahoy!
3. Nabisco Double Stuf Oreo
4. Pepperidge Farm Milano
5. Private label chocolate chip cookies
6. Little Debbie Nutty Bars
7. Little Debbie Oatmeal Creme Pies
8. Nabisco Chips Ahoy! Chewy
9. Nabisco Nilla Wafers
10. Private label sandwich cookies

Coca-Cola

The date was May 8, 1886.

The Civil War had been over for twenty-one years.

Grover Cleveland was president of the United States.

And in Atlanta, Georgia, a pharmacist named John Pemberton was busy in his backyard. Pemberton had already invented French Wine Coca—"The Ideal Nerve Tonic, Health Restorer and Stimulant," Lemon and Orange Elixir, and Dr. Pemberton's Indian Queen Magic

Hair Dye. But he wanted to invent a remedy for people who imbibed too much.

Using a boat oar to stir, Pemberton cooked up a mixture in a brass kettle heated over an open fire. When he finished, he had a new medicine to relieve exhaustion, aid the nervous, and soothe headaches.

Pemberton took his new medicine to the Jacobs Pharmacy. He instructed Venable, his assistant, to mix the syrup with water and chill it with ice. They tasted it and agreed it was delicious. But when Venable mixed another glass, he accidentally added carbonated water instead of plain water.

This time the men became excited. They decided that instead of offering the beverage as a headache remedy, they would sell it as a fountain drink—an alternative to ginger ale and root beer. They named it Coca-Cola after the coca leaves and cola nuts it contained.

In 1886, Coca-Cola sales averaged nine drinks a day. According to the Coca-Cola Company, Pemberton sold twenty-five gallons of syrup that first year. He took in $50 but spent $73.96 on advertising.

Today, nearly 10,450 soft drinks manufactured by Coca-Cola are consumed every second of every day, including Diet Coke, Fanta, and Sprite.

FUN FACTS ABOUT COKE!

Coca-Cola is the second most widely understood term in the world, after "okay."

According to the Coca-Cola Company, if all the Coke ever produced were placed in twelve-ounce cans and stacked in single columns the height of Mount Everest, it would take nineteen million columns of cans to hold the Coke.

The Coca-Cola Facebook page has over ninety million fans and continues to grow.

Doughnut Holes

Hanson Gregory was born in 1832 in Camden, Maine, and died in 1921. He is buried in the Sailors' Snug Harbor Cemetery in Quincy, Massachusetts. During the eighty-nine years that Hanson Gregory lived, he spent many of them as a sea captain. A legend says he was at sea when he invented the doughnut hole.

One night he was eating a fried cake when a violent storm suddenly arose. Captain Gregory needed both hands to steer the ship, so he shoved the cake onto one of the spokes of the ship's helm to keep it safe. Without thinking, he invented the doughnut hole.

When Captain Gregory realized what he had invented, he was pleased. The centers of the fried cakes were always unpleasantly soggy, so removing the center definitely improved the cake. After the storm, the captain ordered the ship's cook to begin making fried cakes with a hole in the middle.

Another, less interesting story says that when Gregory was fifteen, he was watching his mother make fried cakes. Since he disliked the soggy centers, he simply suggested she remove them. Mrs. Gregory tried her son's idea and it worked.

Today, experts estimate that $11.6 billion worth of doughnut holes are sold each year. That's a lot of holes!

Fudge

One definition of the noun "fudge" is "nonsense or foolishness." And that's how our favorite chocolate candy got its name.

A story says that in the 1890s, a candymaker in Philadelphia was supervising his employees as they made caramels. Someone made a mistake, and instead of producing a chewy candy, the batch turned into a finely crystallized, nonchewy substance.

"Fudge!" the candymaker swore. And with that exclamation to describe the mistake, fudge was born.

Throughout the years, there have been many variations of fudge, but here is a simple recipe:

CREAM CHEESE FUDGE

Recipe

1 six-ounce package semisweet chocolate morsels
2 three-ounce packages cream cheese, softened
4 cups sifted confectioners' sugar
2 tablespoons evaporated milk
1½ teaspoons vanilla
¼ teaspoon salt
2 cups chopped nuts

Melt the chocolate morsels in the top of a double boiler. In a mixing bowl, beat cream cheese until smooth. To the cream cheese, add confectioners' sugar and evaporated milk, and blend. Stir the melted chocolate into the cheese mixture. Stir in the vanilla and salt, then the chopped nuts. Press mixture into a well-greased 9-inch-square pan. Cover and refrigerate overnight.

(Note: Cream Cheese Fudge is a modern recipe and *not* the original "mistake" recipe.)

Ice Cream Cone

The Chinese made iced desserts thousands of years ago, and George Washington was fond of ice cream, but the ice cream cone was not popular until after 1904.

Two food vendors had stands near each other at the 1904 World's Fair in St. Louis. Ernest A. Hamwi, a Syrian who had been in the United States a year, was selling zalabia. Zalabia was a wafer-thin Persian waffle. Nearby, another stand was selling ice cream.

Summer in St. Louis is h-o-t, and the ice cream vendor soon ran out of dishes in which to serve his ice cream. Hamwi quickly rolled one of his waffles into a cone shape and topped it with a scoop of the neighbor's ice cream. The treat was an instant hit and the "World's Fair Cornucopia" became what we know today as the ice cream cone.

While the story of Hamwi's ice cream cone is generally accepted, another man thought a lot like Hamwi. An Italian named Italo Marchiony ran a pushcart business in New York City selling lemon ice in a cone. At first he used a paper cone, then a pastry one.

Marchiony even applied for a patent in September 1903, and received it in December—six months before the St. Louis World's Fair began.

Great minds think alike! Both Hamwi and Marchiony devised the idea for an ice cream cone. But it was probably the large number of people who tasted Hamwi's cones at the St. Louis World's Fair that made the ice cream cone the popular treat we know today.

FUN FACTS ABOUT ICE CREAM!

Hot fudge is the world's most popular ice cream topping.

Chocolate is the #1 flavor of ice cream in the United States.

It takes about fifty licks to finish a single-scoop ice cream cone.

California produces the most ice cream in America.

Maple Syrup

Warm days. Cool nights.

That's the magic formula for sugar maple tree growers. And February through March or April is the magic time to tap the trees. A single maple tree might give from ten to twenty-five gallons of sap.

The history of maple syrup goes back many centuries, and there is a legend about its discovery.

The story says Chief Woksis, an Iroquois, left camp in early March for a day of hunting. As he left, he pulled his tomahawk from the maple tree where he had hurled it the night before. During the day, sap dripped from the tree into a vessel standing close to the tree trunk.

When the evening came, the chief's wife noticed the

"tree water" (which we call sap) in the vessel. She decided to use the tree water to prepare supper and save herself a trip to the spring. As it cooked, the sap boiled down into a syrup. When Chief Woksis arrived home, he was delighted with the new maple flavor of his supper.

Native Americans called the sweetener maple water, and as early explorers and settlers arrived in North America, they taught the white man how to process maple syrup.

Modern technology has improved the sap-gathering process as well as the evaporation method. But no one can improve on the natural goodness of real maple syrup.

About the Author

Charlotte Foltz Jones was an author of award-winning nonfiction books for children, as well as numerous magazine articles. She collaborated with John O'Brien on *Eat Your Words* and *Mistakes That Worked*.

About the Illustrator

John O'Brien is well-known for his *New Yorker* magazine cartoons, as well as his numerous children's book illustration credits, including *Eat Your Words* and *Mistakes That Worked*.